Social Media Marketing For Beginners

How to Build a Social Media Strategy That Really Works

Table of Contents

Introduction

I want to thank you and congratulate you for downloading the book, Social Media Marketing for Beginners.

This book contains proven steps and strategies on how to use social media to promote your business, retain customers, build loyalty, and attract new business.

What is social media? Why and how should you use it to grow your business? How do you know if it's working for you? Social media is a fast-moving platform, constantly growing and changing, and it has immense power to help you advertise and build your business. Using it for marketing, however, can seem like a monumental task for a small business. This book cuts that task down to size, giving you solid advice in simple steps, so that you too can begin to expand product awareness, grow sales, and increase customer loyalty.

Thanks again for downloading this book, I hope you enjoy it!

Chapter 1 - Social Media: what and why?

Social media is any platform where people interact to create and share ideas, opinions, or graphics in a virtual community or network. It began in 1994 with Geocities, but it has grown exponentially in the 20 years since then. Increased usage of the Internet has given birth to an astounding array of social media venues. Now widespread use of smartphones has brought mobile social media into the mix. Social media is immediate; it's visual; it's interactive; and, it's fun.

Why is this important to your business? Social media is now the #1 daily activity among Americans. That's right, it's *numero uno*---more than email, surfing the web, or gaming! Look around you at the park or food court. People, especially younger people, are on their phones on social media sites, even when they're sitting with friends! Ask any teacher about the constant battle they wage to keep students' attention in the classroom and off the social media. Social interaction is coming to mean social media interaction.

Studies have also found that almost 80% of people rely on their social networks both for information and for recommendations about products and services. They trust their social networks, but less than 15% trust advertisements! Join the network and get honest reviews and recommendations from real people. Companies such as Angie's List have been built their whole business around this simple fact.

Social media marketing includes using blogs, content sites, and networking sites to attract and keep customers. Just for big businesses? No. Many small businesses actually do better with social media than large companies do. Social media is about people, and small businesses can often do that much better than many large corporate entities can. It's a shift in marketing thinking, and it's about listening to and interacting with customers and potential customers. Individuals and smaller businesses do that every day; the VP of Marketing at X Corporation, not so much! According to Fast Company, social media is used by 93% of all marketers. Think that may include your competition? You bet!

So, how does the average person get started using social media marketing? First, there are a few things to know up front. Social media is not free, not for marketing well, since you'll need to buy ads, etc. It's also not a quick fix marketing tool, and it cannot overcome poor products or poor service. It's not a magic wand. That said, before getting involved in social media you need to understand what's out there. Facebook and Twitter are just the tip of the iceberg! Recent figures rank the top 15 social networking sites as follows:

- Facebook

- Twitter

- LinkedIn

- Pinterest

- Google Plus+

- Tumblr

- Instagram

- VK

- Flickr

- Vine

- Meetup

- Tagged

- Ask.fm

- Meet Me

- Classmates

Wow! You're probably familiar with some of those, and you've never heard of some of the others. That's OK. Do some research on the various sites. Find out how they work. Some are slower paced than others; some are totally image-driven. What type of social media best suits both you and your business? Think about that, and then move on to Chapter 2, Strategy!

Chapter 2 - Strategy: making a realistic plan

Using the social media for marketing has been described as a marathon, not a sprint. You need to start slowly, pace yourself, and have the patience and endurance to hang in there for the long haul. This is particularly true for those without previous marketing experience! Using the social media to promote your business can be confusing, frustrating, and a waste of your precious time and money unless you have a game plan before you start the race. So the first step to planning a strategy that will work for you is to answer a few basic questions about your product, business, or service.

Who are you?

It's very important in social media marketing to "know thyself". You know what you're marketing, sure, but you need to look deeper. What's your pitch? Can you describe your business in 120 characters or less? Try it! You'll need to be clear and concise to function well in social media. What makes you, your product, and your business different? Can you sum it up in one word? Volvo=safety. Hallmark=heart. What do you equal? The answers to these questions will be your guidepost in your social media marketing. It's about BEING social, not DOING social. You're not appealing to the heads but rather the hearts of your audience. You need to be human, to act like a person not a company. No, you won't need to put cute puppies out there (unless that's YOU)! Knowing who you are and what image you want to project will help you in selecting your social media channels as well as your content. So, be honest and think!

What are your goals?

Why are you thinking of using social media for marketing? The "why" will determine the "how", so you need to clarify your purpose before you begin. Where are you now, and where do you want to go? Building awareness is the first level, so decide if this is where you need to start. Do people know who, what, and where you are? Check the reviewing sites? How are people seeing your business and their experiences with you? If you have negative answers here, then you need to raise public awareness of your business. If the public generally knows about you, then increasing sales is the next step. After that would come customer retention or loyalty. You cannot measure whether your social media marketing is effective if you don't clearly understand your primary goal and how it may change over time.

Who's your audience?

Who are your current customers? You need to understand the demographics involved because different groups (age, ethnicity, economic status, etc.) use technology and social media differently. Older people, for instance, may post on Facebook but they may not Tweet. So first define your customers; then find out how they're using social media. A Social Technographics Ladder is a great tool for helping you with this, and a simple web search can help you find it! Are your customers mainly creators or joiners? This will help you to choose the "how" for implementing your social media marketing strategy. The second important question here is: who are your desired customers? If you want to grow your customer base (and sales), you need to know not just what type of new customers you want but also how to connect with them. How are they using social media differently from your current customers?

Once you have the answers to these questions, you've basically formulated your strategy. You have a clear understanding of what you're selling, what your goal is, and who your target group is and how to reach them. You've dealt with the hard part! Now to put your plan into action!

Chapter 3 - Implementation: How to get started

Remember the marathon analogy? Don't sprint off establishing a presence on 10 different social media sites! Warm up, pace yourself, and keep your goal in view. The first phase of implementation is to do a little research. Your competitors can help guide you to the areas where you should be active, so check out what they're doing on social media and evaluate it. What are your customers saying? Where are they saying it? Listen to them. Brainstorm about what kind of marketing you need to focus on first. Be creative!

Your information from your customers, combined with what your competition is doing, should lead you to the type of social media you need to start with. There are two main types: social platforms and social networks. Social platforms are channels such as blogs, podcasts, or YouTube. They are a place to establish your expertise and build your credibility. You can engage in discussion, answer questions, and get valuable feedback. Networks, on the other hand, are channels such as Facebook, Twitter, or LinkedIn. They are more like a live networking event and can be used to build customer relationships and contacts. Both serve different purposes in marketing via social media.

You may want to first register on many channels to secure your company handle and set up minimal branding so you'll have consistency in your name across the channels. This way your customers can find you easily. This doesn't mean you're going to be active on all of them---not yet! Most experts suggest you start small and go deep. Choose one from each broad type of social media, hopefully one where your customers are active. If you already have a Facebook page, start there and then add a blog. Only you can decide which channels would be best for you and your business. An artist and a plumber will have much different needs! But, pick two---that's the "start small".

The "go deep" part of the experts' advice means you really need to learn how to use those two channels, mine them for all their worth. Master them before you even think about adding another. Come up with a game plan for your activity on those channels. You need to be active, but you also need to set realistic goals and meet them! Start with easily attainable goals: "I'll do 4 tweets a day and a new blog entry once a week." OK, stick with it for several weeks. Are those goals working for you? If you could easily add more, then raise your goals slightly, but stay realistic! Starting too strong can overwhelm you with social media obligations and distractions and take you away from your actual work. Take it slow, easy, and always follow your game plan. This is the marathon part. You want to establish a presence on social media, a presence that is credible and reliable, so your customers and potential customers will become fans and followers!

Chapter 4 - Content: making customers your best ad agents

The single thing that will make your social media marketing ultimately successful is its quality. You need to establish high standards and provide high quality content. Don't count on having your tweet go viral! It would be nice, but it's not very likely. What will convert your customers into followers, fans, and free advertising agents for you, is what you put out there. High quality social media marketing embraces two main areas: content and visuals.

Content is particularly important on social platform channels, such as YouTube, blogging, podcasting, and Slide Share, but also on your web site. You want to provide a resource for customers, one that offers valid and valuable content. One expert recommends that you strive to be the "go-to" resource in your industry. Provide lots of free but relevant information because everyone loves free. Get into the "they ask, you answer" mindset. Establish your expertise and build your credibility as an expert in your field. What helpful advice can you offer or procedure can you explain?

Let's take a detailed example here. Saturday night I throw my dogs in the tub and give them thorough baths.

All clean and lovely! I'm happy, even if they're not. That is, I'm happy until I hop in the shower Sunday morning and end up with water backed up to above my ankles! Argh! It's Sunday, I have a badly clogged drain, and I'm no plumber. What do I do? I Google it, of course, to see if someone who knows about this stuff can point me in the right direction for a solution. I get a hit: removing hair from bathtub drain. YES! If this article is helpful and honest, I'll not only return to this page in the future but also recommend it to friends in need. I may "like" them on Facebook and post about how they helped me out of a jam. And, if I can't solve this on my own---all the suggestions fail and I'm told I'll really need a plumber--- guess who I'll call if they're local? Exactly. I do it, you do it, and everyone does it! I've gone back and posted positive feedback when someone's blog has helped me get my DVD working again or enabled me to inexpensively repair a doorknob. Build that content for your industry...and they will come.

You can reuse your content on different channels by customizing its format for that channel. Remember that the channels appeal to different types and demographics of users, so you need to adapt your content across channels. LinkedIn, for instance, is business focused and its users like in-depth content. Instagram is predominantly visual, and Facebook posts are different from both. Also, use the search function in the channel to see if there are groups talking about your industry or some related topic and join in. Become a member of industry relevant groups within the channel, if you can, and take part in open discussions as they arise. If what you contribute is good, you'll get noticed. Another good tool is Google alerts, which can let you know both when and where you can join relevant discussions. These conversations can keep you current and in touch with industry trends or concerns, as well as establishing you as a knowledgeable person in your field.

One warning on content, however, has to do with that "high quality" requirement. Your content must be well written (or well filmed for YouTube). Misspellings, typos, and grammar errors (or bad lighting and watery sound) are going to seriously detract from your credibility as a professional. So, if you have great ideas and can explain things clearly but are not so hot with the grammar, get help BEFORE YOU POST. I know people whose Facebook posts are chock full of misspellings (and you do too), and, if they're teachers, for instance, it strikes a sour note. If you don't have someone readily available to proofread and edit for you, hire someone! If you take terrible blurry photos, hire someone! It's less expensive than you think, and you may already have friends and neighbors who are good at these things. They'd love to pick up a little extra cash and help you out. Also, freelancers can be hired both online and locally to help you quickly and expertly produce quality content. We're all good at different things, so reach out for help to keep your content high quality!

This leads us to the visual aspect of content. Of course, anything you upload to YouTube should be not only good quality but also appropriate to your industry. It can be funny or serious, but it should never be shoddy. "Appropriate" varies widely by industry, obviously, and what's OK for an escort service to put out there would never do for the local church to upload, even if it's hilarious! Videos on your web site or linked to your blog are tremendous, but do it well! If you've reposting it from elsewhere, acknowledge that and credit the source. Again, see what your competitors are doing, and then do it better!

Visuals, however, involve more than video. Every graphic you use should be high quality, clear, and preferably yours. Stock photos are wonderfully done...but they're not you! Authentic photos are the best because social media is about connecting. Take good photos of your business and invite your customers to share theirs. Also learn a little about editing your photos since most can be greatly improved by some easy minor fixes. There are some great free tutorials online to show you the basics, and it's not difficult once you know the tricks. Both the written and visual content of your social media marketing will stand as an example of the standards that you follow in your business.

Have you noticed that "selling" has not come into this discussion of content? There's a good reason for that! One of the content guidelines in social media is "Tell, don't sell". The old "hard sell" has no place in this strategy. It's a **connection** you're looking for in using social media ... friendship, trust and respect. You're a person, not a disembodied corporate entity, and your present and future customers will connect with that. The rest will follow.

Chapter 5 - Customer Service: growing fans and followers

Customer service goes hand in hand with high quality content in successful social media marketing. It's all about being social with those customers...and keeping their business. Blogging, tweeting, and posting are great, but you need to listen even more. Social media is a conversation, and you need to give your customers the opportunity to speak and then to listen carefully to what they have to say.

What do they want? How could you improve what you do, or offer them something more they could use? Ask them! That's seems simple, but it an often overlooked business tool. Just ask...ask them about their needs, their experiences with your business, their photos...just ask! Like them on Facebook; join the tweeting on what's the best Chinese restaurant; don't just ask them to follow you. It's a two-way street! By engaging in social media marketing, you're inviting them to your party, so get the conversation going or it'll be a social disaster. Too many people begin social media marketing and just blog, blog, blog. They don't listen. You must listen or you're wasting your time! Don't be that boring guy who spends the whole party trying to sell you insurance! Ask your customers about anything, join their conversations, comment on their posts, and be social. Social media marketing is all about interaction!

No, not all you're going to hear about your business will make you happy. And, yes, some of it may surprise you. Social media is a huge opportunity to show everyone how well you treat your customers, and it's equally an opportunity to turn a bad customer experience around. Don't ignore any comments, positive or negative. Response is imperative! This is another reason you don't want to jump into too many ponds to start with, because you need to keep up with it all and respond! Responding to positive feedback is easy but still necessary, and who doesn't appreciate a simple "Thanks!" Try to use the negative comments as a chance to make things right with that customer if you can. Acknowledge their problem or complaint, and let them know you'll contact them privately to see about resolving the issue. Sometimes just a simple apology can work wonders! Remember that this is all in a public venue so everyone there can see not only THAT you respond, but also HOW you respond. They'll know you're hearing them...you're listening! Remember...this is about connecting.

Apart from the obvious, how can this help your business? How is this "marketing"? Here's what happened with Dave Kerpen, chairman of Likeable Media. He was in Las Vegas, waiting a very long time to get checked in to his hotel. The line was just not moving. So he did what many customers now do---he hopped on Twitter and posted that he'd been waiting on line to check in for 45 minutes (#fail)! Although he didn't get a response from his hotel, within minutes he was tweeted by a hotel down the street, empathizing with his experience and hoping the rest of his visit went better. No, he didn't switch hotels that visit, but he did the next time he went to Vegas! He also "liked" the responsive hotel on Facebook, and a friend who saw that "like" asked him if he'd recommend the hotel, which he did. This is how social media marketing works, and it's why response and patience are important. It's like "The House That Jack Built". Respond, not just to your own customers but also to anyone needing your services or having a bad experience with a competitor. It pays off!

The other aspect of customer service that's relevant here is also shown in the example above. Embrace your mistakes, learn from them, and acknowledge them. Things get goofed up and we all know it! Respond proactively, apologize, and address the issue. If Dave Kerpen had heard from his own hotel, it might have stopped the whole chain of events dead in its tracks...but he didn't. Notice that he didn't get any "sell" from the other hotel, just sympathy and good wishes...and that was enough to bring not just him but several other new customers to their hotel in the long run. And there's that marathon aspect again!

Chapter 6 - Moving forward: tracking and fine-tuning

Once you've made your game plan and put it into action, how do you know if it's working? Linking your areas of activity is important, so use the tools available in each channel to refer people to your other channels and to your web site. Increased site traffic will lead to increased sales. Tracking the response to your activity in social media is vital if you're going to market successfully.

The easiest way to see the results of your efforts is to use tracking software. There's a lot out there, and some very good programs, especially for beginners, are free. Do a search for "social media marketing monitoring analytics and management" and you'll find hundreds of programs. Some are free; some are available in both free and paid versions; and some you'll need to buy. Read about them, including user reviews, to help you find a good match. As a beginner, you don't need fancy bells and whistles, so many of the free programs are not only a great place to start but also are simple to use and understand. Popular software includes bit.ly, Google Analytics, Hootsuite, Icerocket, and Social Mention. Get set up, get tracking, and get the information you need.

You should review your tracking stats monthly, and you need to look at each channel separately. What's been your return on investment (ROI) for each? This is when you need to make adjustments, refocus your efforts, and re-evaluate aspects of your strategy. Those changes can include anything from what channels you're trying to use to the quality of your content to your responsiveness.

Are you putting hours into a blog that's not attracting followers? Be open to considering various options. Is it the content or the writing of your blog that might be the problem? You could search more interesting topics or ask your customers to suggest topics? What do people want to know? Perhaps you need to hire a ghostwriter or copyeditor for your blog to make your content "pop". Or maybe, just maybe, a blog wasn't the best match with your business. Perhaps you need to try a different sort of channel. Are your customers elsewhere? If you can't keep up with the posts or can't respond quickly, could you hire someone to do that for you? It's a great part time job for teen-agers and college students! Keep an open mind and make needed adjustments. Re-evaluate every step of your plan and tweak as needed.

You need to evaluate each social media channel that you're using on a regular basis, and fine-tune your usage of it. Keep a calendar to stay on track with those posting goals that you set, and don't forget that social media builds slowly. Remember to "go deep"---become a master at using that channel! Find tips, tricks, and tutorials to expand and improve how you're using it. There's a wealth of material available on line, from free YouTube how-to's to paid classes in targeted skills.

The other aspect of tracking is to use it to fine-tune your marketing for the particular audience of each channel. You can be more creative and immediate in social media than you can in traditional marketing. Your post is up and received right away, so limited time offers can take on a new meaning! So can coupons on smartphones. You can send out a special offer that's only good for the next hour! And, if it's a great offer, your followers will share the news. You may attract new fans who'll be waiting for that offer the next time around. Think "flash mob"---if you miss the first one, you want to be on the list for the next.

Partnering up with another business for offers is also a social media tactic for creating a buzz in a limited time. There's the story of the partnering of a Mexican food truck with a travel agency. For two hours only (starting now!) anyone getting the BOGO taco special at the truck was eligible to BOGO flights to Mexico at the agency. You'd better believe that the people who got that notice via their social media feeds talked about it! Some took advantage of the offer, and some couldn't or didn't. But they posted about it either way! So be creative with your contests, giveaways, etc. Think outside the box. Just be sure your offers or contests will appeal to your demographic. "Create a new jingle for us" is not going to appeal to all groups, so keep both basic marketing principles and the users of the channel in mind.

Use all the resources available within the channel. Facebook has both ads and offers, and they show up in different places. Create and join groups, sponsor surveys, share humorous comics or posters, link your sites, get on RSS feeds...whatever makes sense for your business and for you.

Another marketing resource is to get and stay active on Google Plus+. If you are actively publishing on that channel, you basically get free ad space when users search for you on Google. This boosts the visibility of your content and your business.

Chapter 7 - And now...

Take a deep breath! We've covered a lot in a few pages. Take some time to go back, reread, assimilate, and clarify your thoughts on each step. Understand how each element is different on social media from the traditional marketing that you're used to. Ask, listen, and learn. Social media marketing can seem like a huge bog just waiting to pull you in, but with planning and clear goals you can stay on firm ground. Start small, go deep, and pace your participation realistically. Go where your customers are. Social media marketing is interaction, and building relationships takes time. But, in the end, the rewards for you and your business will be worth it.

You may be a beginner now, but armed with this basic knowledge you can become adept in no time! So get out there, get your running shoes on, and join the social media marketing marathon! Have fun with it...and don't "do" social, BE SOCIAL!

Conclusion

Thank you again for downloading this book!

I hope this book was able to help you to understand how you too can use the social media to promote your business by increasing your visibility, sparking your sales, and building your customers trust and loyalty.

The next step is to look closely at your business and your customers, set your goals, make your plan, and go for it!

Finally, if you enjoyed this book, then I'd like to ask you for a favor, would you be kind enough to leave a review for this book on Amazon? It'd be greatly appreciated!

Click here to leave a review for this book on Amazon!

http://amzn.to/1wxVw2r

Thank you and good luck!

Check Out My Other Books

Below you'll find some of my other popular books that are popular on Amazon and Kindle as well. Simply click on the links below to check them out.

SEO Basics: How to use Search Engine Optimization (SEO) to take your business to the next level of success

Social Media Marketing for Beginners: How to build a social media strategy that really works

Affiliate Marketing for Beginners: Simple, smart and proven strategies to make A LOT of money online, the easy way

If the links do not work, for whatever reason, you can simply search for these titles on the Amazon website to find them.

This document is geared towards providing exact and reliable information in regards to the topic and issue covered. The publication is sold with the idea that the publisher is not required to render accounting, officially permitted, or otherwise, qualified services. If advice is necessary, legal or professional, a practiced individual in the profession should be ordered.

- From a Declaration of Principles which was accepted and approved equally by a Committee of the American Bar Association and a Committee of Publishers and Associations.

The information provided herein is stated to be truthful and consistent, in that any liability, in terms of inattention or otherwise, by any usage or abuse of any